This Little Yoga book belongs to

. . . . Aith Nursery . . . . .

For Scarlett with love – R.W.

For my granddaughter Mathilda – M.S.

LITTLE YOGA
A HUTCHINSON BOOK 0 09 189349 6

Published in Great Britain by Hutchinson,
an imprint of Random House Children's Books.

This edition published 2005

1 3 5 7 9 10 8 6 4 2

Text copyright © Rebecca Whitford, 2005
Illustrations copyright © Martina Selway, 2005

The right of Rebecca Whitford and Martina Selway to be identified as the author and illustrator
of this work has been asserted in accordance with the Copyright, Designs and Patents Act 1988.

RANDOM HOUSE CHILDREN'S BOOKS,
a division of The Random House Group Ltd,
London, Sydney, Auckland, Johannesburg and agencies throughout the world

THE RANDOM HOUSE GROUP Limited Reg. No. 954009

www.kidsatrandomhouse.co.uk

A CIP catalogue record for this book is available from the British Library.

Printed in Singapore

Little Yoga

A Toddler's
First Book of Yoga

Rebecca Whitford & Martina Selway

HUTCHINSON
LONDON SYDNEY AUCKLAND JOHANNESBURG

Yoga Baby . . .

spreads his arms out like a

flutter flutter

butterfly

hangs down like a

oooh oooh

monkey

Yoga Baby...

breathes like a

haaaaa   haaaaa

lion – 'Haaaa'

Yoga Baby...

stretches like an

miaow
miaow

angry cat

Yoga Baby...

curls up like a

ZZZZZZ
ZZZZZZZ

sleeping mouse

Yoga Baby...

wobbles like a

tweet

tweet

little bird

Yoga Baby . . .

crouches down like a

ribbit *ribbit*

frog

Yoga Baby

says time for a

Z Z Z Z

rest –

'ahh, shh, shh'

Little Yoga

A Note to Parents and Carers

Little Yoga is a gentle and fun introduction to a balanced yoga sequence for toddlers to enjoy — either by copying Yoga Baby and practising with Mum or Dad or to simply read and share. Yoga is a great way for children to develop strength and suppleness, improve physical coordination and mental concentration as well as increasing self-awareness and self-confidence. With practice, yoga can help to calm and relax toddlers by encouraging moments of quiet and stillness.

Toddlers are naturally flexible and will enjoy the animal role-play but may find things like balancing and relaxing more challenging. **Little Yoga** is designed for fun, not as a manual, so allow it to take its own playful form and give your child lots of encouragement.

Practice tips:

- Practise with bare feet on a non-slip surface; use a clear space in a warm room and wear loose, comfortable clothes.

- Like any form of exercise it is best not to practise this sequence immediately after eating.

- Practise with your child so that he or she can copy you.

- Use your own judgement with your child's ability and let your child move at his or her own pace, giving support where necessary.

- Encourage your child into poses but do not look for or expect perfection. Most of all **Little Yoga** is meant to be a fun, positive experience.

- Don't force your toddler into a pose or let him or her hold any pose for too long.

- Allow your child to play around with a pose before moving on to the next one.

- Encourage your child to keep his or her breath flowing — toddlers are too young to know when to inhale and exhale — and to move slowly in and out of the poses.

- Discourage your child from taking any weight onto his or her head (they are tempted to do this in the Downward Dog pose), and be ready to catch your Yoga Baby when balancing!

- Simple stories can help your Yoga Baby relax when in the resting pose.

- The photos overleaf are not precise because they are a real reflection of how our toddlers have interpreted the poses!

Most importantly, keep your **Little Yoga** practice **Simple, playful** and **fun!**

Explanation of Poses

Butterfly (Flying Eagle) – from a standing position raise arms out and up. Stretch up while coming up on tiptoes. Lower arms to the sides and come down slowly onto feet. It may help to practise arm movements before trying tiptoes.

Monkey (Forward Bend) – from standing raise arms in front from the sides, then bend from the waist, letting upper body, arms and hands relax towards the floor. Keep knees bent if more comfortable. Uncurl slowly back to a standing position.

Lion (Lion Breath) – start with a cross-legged, straight-backed, sitting position with hands resting on knees. Breathe in, then breathe out with a loud 'Haaa' sound while sticking the tongue out as far as possible and stretching arms out in front with fingers spread. Some toddlers can also look up to the space between their eyebrows!

Cat – a) from all fours, knees directly under hips, legs parallel, wrists directly under shoulders, tilt the pelvis while moving the chest out, lifting the chin and looking up;
b) tuck bottom in, arch the back so that it is rounded, and relax the head. Repeat both poses as a continuous movement.

Dog (Downward Dog) – from all fours, tuck toes under onto the floor and lift hips and bottom up, push heels down towards the floor, push away from the floor through the palms and relax the head and neck. Come down onto all fours.

Mouse (Pose of a Child) – from all fours, put legs together and sink hips/bottom back towards the feet, forehead to the floor. Try to keep spine in a straight line. Lay arms alongside legs and turn the palms up. Hold and relax.

Bird (Tree Balance) – from standing, bring hands into prayer position in front of chest and take weight onto left leg. Raise right heel to rest on left ankle, toes on the floor and right knee out to the side. When balanced, lift hands in prayer position above head and stretch up. Release foot to the floor and repeat on the other side. It helps to practise against a wall. Once balanced it may be possible to bring the foot further up the inside of the leg, keeping the knee out to the side.

Frog (Squat) – stand with feet at least hip-width apart, toes turned out. Squat down, putting hands on the floor between the knees, directly under the shoulders. Try to keep a straight spine with head and spine in line.

Rest (Savasana) – lie down on back, keeping body in a straight line. Have legs hip-width apart and let feet relax out to the sides. Keep arms away from the body, and the palms turned up. Try to keep head in line with the spine and close the eyes. Imagine sinking into a cloud . . .

Monkey (Forward Bend)

Butterfly (Flying Eagle)

a) Cat

Lion (Lion Breath)

b) Cat

Dog (Downward Dog)

Bird (Tree Balance)

Mouse (Pose of a Child)

Frog (Squat)

Rest (Savasana)